Mrs. Webster's Dictionary

By
Lisa Cofield, Debbie Dingerson,
Maia Lacher, and Lea Rush

Great Quotations Publishing Company
Glendale Heights, Illinois

1

Cover Design & Typesetting: Bostrom Publishing

Published in Glendale Heights, Illinois by Great Quotations Publishing Company

Great Quotations Publishing Company
1967 Quincy Court
Glendale Heights, IL 60139

Printed in Hong Kong

The authors (Lisa Cofield, Debbie Dingerson,
Maia Lacher, and Lea Rush) wish to thank
their family and friends for their support,
patience and sense of humor.

*I*n 1831, Mr. Webster published the first dictionary of the English language. Unfortunately, he omitted several definitions - mostly those related to the daily lives of women. Now, Mrs. Webster is graciously correcting this oversight, making her publishing debut with her own dictionary. She hopes you enjoy it.

–The Authors

Aaaack (aak) *interj*
An utterance upon running directly into
a spider web first thing in the morning
— and you don't know where the spider
is now.

Acne (ak•nee) *n*
A condition you thought was supposed
to disappear after your teen years, but
really doesn't.

Advice (ad•vis) *n*
Opinion or guidance that applies
perfectly to someone else.

Airhead (er•hed) *n*
What a woman intentionally becomes
when pulled over by a policeman.

Mrs. Webster's Dictionary

All-nighters (al•ni•ters) *n*
An activity you do with term papers
during college and children
during parenthood.

Mrs. Webster's Dictionary

Argument (ar•gyou•ment) *n*
A discussion that occurs when you're
right, but he just hasn't realized it yet.

Bachelor (batch•a•ler) *n*
an eligible man who:
- a) is unmarried
- b) is not living with a woman (or in some cases another man)
- c) is not seriously dating
- d) your best friend has no claim to

Bad Hair Day (fri•zee) *n*
A condition now recognized by the AMA
and characterized by "wildly disordered
hair that stands straight out from the
scalp and is resistant to combing."

Balance the Checkbook
(bal•ens da chek•buk) *v*
To go to the cash machine and
hit "inquire."

Mrs. Webster's Dictionary

Bar-be-que (bar•bi•q) *n*
You bought groceries, washed lettuce, chopped tomatoes, diced onions, marinated meat and cleaned everything up, but he "made dinner."

14

Baseball Bat (bas•bol bat) *n.*
An anti-burglar device.

Best Friend (best frend) *n*
1) Someone who ignores the good-
    looking hunk you saw first, and
2) Someone who tells you when your
    skirt is caught in the back of
    your nylons.

Birth Control (burth kon•troll) *n*
See "Kids."

Blonde Jokes (blond joks) *n*
Jokes that are short so men can
understand them.

Blind Date (blind daat) *n*

1) The only thing worse than staying
   home on a Saturday night, or
2) an outing you go on once a year, or
   however long it takes you to forget
   how bad the last one was.

Blue (blu) *n*
Mr. Webster says "a color on the
spectrum between green and violet."
Mrs. Webster agrees, but would like to
differentiate this color from royal, navy,
midnight, etc., thus the need for so
many shoes.

Bra (brah) *n*
A piece of clothing you can't wait to get,
then spend the rest of your life trying to
figure out how to do without.

Bridal Magazine (bri•dull mag•a•zeen) *n*
A publication that prints the same
information month after month, but you
buy ten of them anyway.

Broomstick (broom•stik) *n*
The "other car" of his ex-girlfriend.

Mrs. Webster's Dictionary

Brown (broun) *adj*
The color he cannot distinguish from
blue and black when he puts his socks on.

Bubble Bath (bu•bel bath) *n*
An activity guaranteed to cause the phone
to ring.

Budget (buj•it) *n*
A plan that looks great on paper, but is
fudged in practice. See "Diet."

Camping (kamp•cng) *v*
He wants to immerse himself in the great
outdoors — then the great outdoors
immerses itself in your hair, clothes,
and food.

Cantaloupe (kant•e•lope) *n*
Gotta get married in a church.

Casserole (kass•a•roll) *n*
From the French verb meaning "to use up
leftovers," a main dish usually containing
tuna and topped by crushed potato chips.

Celery (sel•er•ee) *n*
A vegetable used to hold up peanut
butter or cream cheese spread.

Children (chil•dren) *n*
What men become when they get the flu.

Chocolate (chok•o•let) *n*
One of the four food groups.

Chocolate Chip Cookie Dough
(yum•mee) *n*
A substance that never makes it to
the oven.

Classical Music (klas•i•kel mu•zik) *n*
Songs that existed before they were used
in Warner Brother's cartoons.

Closet Space (klo•zit space) *n*
No matter how much you have, there is
never enough. See "Wishful Thinking."

Clothes (kloz) *n*
Something else you never have enough
of. See "Closet Space."

Clothes Dryer (kloze dri•yer) *n*
An appliance designed to eat socks.

Coffee (kof•fee) *n*
A liquid you spill on yourself the first
time you wear a brand new white blouse.

Cold Feet (kold feet) *n*

Mr. Webster: What he got just before getting married.

Mrs. Webster: What she puts on Mr. Webster since getting married.

Comb (kom) *n*
From the same root as "combat," thus "I
have to comb my hair" and "I have to
combat my hair" mean the same thing.

Commitment (ka•mit•ment) *n*
What you decide you're ready for after
the break-up.

Common Knowledge (kom•an nol•ij) *n*
A source cited for a fact you just
made up.

Computer (kom•pew•ter) *n*
The one thing in a woman's life that does
exactly what she tells it to.

Credit Limit (kre•dit lim•it) *n*
How much a credit card company will
let you charge before they cut you off.
In reality, shouldn't this be called a
debt limit??

Date (ra•zin) *n*
If you like him, it's a date. If you're not
sure, it's "just going to dinner."

Dating Service (dat•ing ser•vis) *n*
What you pay good money to join one
month before meeting the man of your
dreams on a street corner.

Diet Soda (dy•it so•da) *n*
A drink you buy at a convenience store
to go with a half-pound bag of
peanut M&Ms.

Directions (di•rek•shuns) *n*
What Mr. Webster:
a) doesn't ask for when he's lost, and
b) rarely follows when he has them.

Dishwasher (dish•wash•er) *n*
The appliance your family puts the
dirty dishes next to so it's easier for you
to load.

Divorce (di•vors) *n*
Archaic. The new politically correct term
is "matrimonially challenged."

Dog (dawg) *n*
A creature who hears a burglar, barks
once, then hides in the closet.

Dutch Treat (cheep) *n*
If he suggests it, dump him. If you sug-
gest it, and he insists on paying anyway,
marry him.

Ecstasy (ex•ta•see) *n*
Bubble bath, chocolate and a trashy
romance novel, preferably all at the
same time.

Engagement Ring (rock) *n*
Something you want to be surprised with,
but also want to help pick out.

Eternity (e•ter•ni•tee) *n*
The last two minutes of a football game.

Exercise (ex•er•siz) *v*
To walk up and down a mall, occasionally
resting to make a purchase.

Fantasy (fan•ta•see) *n*
The belief that marriage or kids will
"change him."

Fiction (fik•shun) *n*
The story your teenager tells you after
arriving home an hour late.

Mrs. Webster's Dictionary

First Date (furst date) *n*
One of the times you should never
order tacos, spaghetti, BBQ or anything
else spillable.

Flowers (flou•ers) *n*
Mr. Webster thinks giving these to Mrs.
Webster will "make up" their fight. Mrs.
Webster says these will help, but he still
has to say he's sorry.

Four Food Groups (for food groops) *n*
Chocolate, wine coolers, potato chips and
ice cream.

Fridays (fry•days) *n*
The night you can finally go out and
play, but are too tired to enjoy.

Friends (frendz) *n*
With "let's be," a polite way of saying
"no, I won't go out with you again."

Golf (galf) *n*

A game in which men spend hours trying to get a little ball into a hole from far away. Why they have the patience to do this, but not to separate your white blouse from their red underwear before putting them in the washing machine is not understood.

Mrs. Webster's Dictionary

Gossip (gah•sip) *n*
A harmless pastime, unless it's about you.

Gourmet Cook (gor•may kook) *n*
Someone with way too much time on
their hands.

Gray Hair (gra hare) *n*
Mrs. Webster wants to believe this doesn't exist, and is willing to pay big bucks so others will also believe it doesn't exist.

Grocery List (grow•ser•ee list) *n*
What you spend half-an-hour writing,
then forget to take with you to the store.

Grocery Shopping
(grow•ser•ee shah•ping) *n*
You go in looking for bread, milk and
eggs, but come out with chocolate, ice
cream and Soap Opera Digest.

Groom (groom) *v, n*
Mr. Webster defines a groom as a verb,
"to train, as for a specific position." Mrs.
Webster defines a groom as a noun, "a
person to train, as for a specific position."

Hair Dresser (harc dres•cr) *n*
Someone who is able to create a style you
will never be able to duplicate again.
See "Magician."

Hair Spray (hare spra) *n*
A substance you spend 15 minutes
applying to your hair to achieve 5
minutes of hold.

Halloween (hal•o•ween) *n*
A chance to wear the outfit you bought,
but were too embarrassed to wear any
other time.

Handsome (han•sum) adj

Harry Belefonte	Ricardo Montelban
Pierce Brosnan	Paul Newman
Sean Connery	Sidney Poitier
Tom Cruise	Robert Redford
Timothy Dalton	Christopher Reeves
Kirk Douglas	Tom Selleck
Harrison Ford	Jimmy Smits
Clark Gable	Patrick Stewart
Richard Gere	Patrick Swayze
Mel Gibson	Denzel Washington
Cary Grant	Billy Dee Williams
James Earl Jones	your husband
A Martinez	

Hardware Store (hard•war stor) *n*
Similar to a black hole in space — if
he goes in, he isn't coming out
anytime soon.

High Heels (hi heelz) *n*
1) A method of torture disguised as a
   fashion statement.
2) A tool designed to be used as a
   hammer (see also screwdriver).
3) A lawn aerator.

Home (hom) *n*
A dwelling that ideally has the same
number of bathrooms as people.

Honeymoon (hun•ee•moon) *n*
A vacation during which you spend
the first three days recovering from
the wedding.

Housewife (howse•wif) *n*
Full time job with non-paid labor, no sick
leave, no vacation benefits, no overtime
pay, and no union representatives.

Idealist (i•de•el•ist) *n*
A woman who believes a romance novel
will come true.

Idunno (i•dun•no)
The person who broke Mrs. Webster's
favorite vase.

Ironing (i•er•ning) *n*
The chore directly responsible for "the wrinkled look."

Jeans (jeenz) *n*
Blue: Casual wear.
Black: Formal wear.

Kiss (kis) *n*
A small token of affection,
usually chocolate.

Jewelry (joo•el•ree) *n*
An all-purpose gift given to women,
similar to ties for men and preferred
over blenders.

Labor (la•ber) *n*
You get to go through 36 hours of
contractions; he gets to hold your
hand and say "focus, breathe, push."

Labor Day (la•ber dae) *n*
A holiday when Mr. and Mrs. Webster
celebrate the kids going back to school.

Laundry (lon•dree) *n*
Dirty clothes that multiply when left in
the hamper overnight.

Life (lif) *n*
Begins when the kids leave home.

Lipstick (lip•stik) *n*
On your lips, coloring to enhance the beauty of your mouth. On his collar, coloring only a tramp would wear.

Mrs. Webster's Dictionary

Logical (loj•i•cal) *adj*
Mr. Webster says "showing consistency of reasoning." Mrs. Webster likes this definition and uses the following sentence as an example: "It's OK to eat chocolate ice cream and potato chips since I walked to the grocery store to buy them."

Makeup (mak•up) *n*
What we spend two hours putting on to
achieve the "natural look."

Mall (maul) *n*

1) A place even women with no sense of direction can find their way around, and

2) A single woman's "home away from home."

Mask (maask) *n*
Green or blue stuff you have all over your
face when your handsome neighbor
comes over to "borrow a cup of sugar."

Men's Sale (minz sal) *n*
It's OK to get one on sale, just make sure
the store has a good return policy.

Microwave (mi•kro•wav) *n*
The greatest time saving invention since
the washing machine.

Mother's Day (muth•crz dac) *n*
A day you agonize more over what to give
his mother than your own.

Mousse (moos) *n*
1) A heavenly chocolate dessert.
2) Foam used on hair to achieve longer hold.
Do not confuse the two.

Music (mu•zik) *n*
An age measuring device; you know
you're getting old when your favorite
songs are "golden oldies."

Nail (nal) *n*
Mr. Webster says a nail is something you hit with a hammer. Mrs. Webster agrees, and is annoyed because she has to re-do her manicure.

Nap (naap) *n*
What you send the kids to take so you
can get some rest.

Needlepoint (nee•dl•point) *n*
A project you start as a wedding gift
for a friend, but give to her for her
tenth anniversary.

New Age (noo aj) *n*
The age a woman gives instead of her real age.

New Year's (noo yeerz) *n*
The time of the year when women feel
even more compelled to set unreasonable
goals for themselves.

Occupant (auk•u•pant) *n*
The person who receives most of the
mail, but never pays any of the bills.

Oops (oops) *interj*
A phrase that should immediately be
followed by a reassurance that everything
is under control.

Opinion (o•pin•yen) *n*
Advice you get whether you ask for it
or not.

Optical Illusion (op•ti•kal i•loo•zhen) *n*
Why most women wear vertical stripes
instead of horizontal ones.

Orthodontist (tooth dok•ter) *n*
A major shareholder in your children.

Panty Hose (pan•tee hoz) *n*
The cheap ones last forever; the
expensive ones snag as you take them
out of the package.

Park (park) *v, n*
Before children, a verb meaning "to go
somewhere and neck."
After children, a noun meaning a place
with a swing set and slide.

Patience (pa•shens) *n*
The most important ingredient for
dating, marriage and children. See
also "tranquilizers."

Peanut Butter (pe•nut but•er) *n*
A basic staple of children's lunches and
single women's meals.

Penny Nail (pen•nee nal) *n*
Archaic. Mrs. Webster says these don't
exist — hers cost at least $30.

Peripheral Vision (pe•rif•er•al vizh•en) *n*
The ability to see what your children are
doing, even if they're at the opposite end
of the house.

Permanent (pur•ma•nent) *n*
Curls that are only temporary, unless it's a
bad perm — those last forever.

Personality (pur•sen•al•a•tee) *n*
If your best friend says your blind date
has a good one, you're in trouble.

Pill (pill) *n*
Women refer to only one thing as a pill.
Everything else is "medicine."

Pizza (peet•za) *n*
An excellent breakfast food.

Plumber (plum•mer) *n*
Call this person after your resident Mr.
Fix-it says "Oh, honey, I'll take care of
that leaky faucet myself."

PMS (pee em es) *n*
Archaic. The new politically correct term
is "hormonally challenged."

Politician (pol•i•tish•en) *n*
Someone who begs for your vote for six
months, then ignores your issues for
four years.

Pregnancy (preg•nan•see) *n*
You gain 30 lbs of water weight, but he
says "we're pregnant."

Procrastination (pro•kras•ti•na•shen) *n*
We'll get to this one later.

Puppy (pup•ee) *n*
An accessory men use to meet women
in the park — sometimes the cuter of
the two.

Purse (purs) *n*
A large bag containing everything except
the item you're looking for.

Remote Control (re•mot kon•troll) *n*
The scepter of power in the household.
"She holds the remote control in the fam
ily" may now be substituted for "She
wears the pants in the family."

Retirement (re•tir•ment) *n*
What Mrs. Webster can't enjoy because
Mr. Webster is always underfoot.

Reunion (re•yoon•yen) *n*
In theory, a time to see old friends. In
practice, a time to try to impress people
you haven't seen in 10 years.

Romance Novel (ro•mans nov•el) *n*
A completely believable story in which an
arrogant, boorish, rude, cold-hearted cad
by day turns into a sensitive, caring,
thoughtful, passionate lover by night. See
also "Idealist."

Run (run) *n*
Mr. Webster: a score in baseball.
Mrs. Webster: a long snag that appears
in panty hose right before the most
important meeting of her life.

Salary (sal•a•ree) *n*
You get two-thirds of what he makes, but do twice the work.

Sale (sail) *n*
Where you spend twice your clothing
budget, but justify it by "all the money
you saved." See also "logical."

Saturday Morning Cartoons
(Bugz Bun•ee) *n*
What you turn on "for the kids" — even
if you don't have children.

Mrs. Webster's Dictionary

Screwdriver (skrew•dri•ver) *n*
A hardware tool designed to be turned
around and used as a hammer.

Selective Hearing (tun•u•out) *n*
The phenomenon by which he will not
hear you from two feet away, but will
respond to the grandchildren from three
rooms away.

Self Cleaning (self klen•eng) *adj*
Ovens are. Floors, windows, dishes and
clothes are not, contrary to the belief of
most husbands and children.

Sex (seks) *n*
An activity your parents want to pretend you don't know about until you are 45 years old and have 3 kids.

Sharing (shar•eng) *v*
1) What he thinks he's doing when he
   leaves you one cookie in the bottom of
   a freshly opened box, and
2) What he swears he does with the
   sheets and blankets.

Sheet Marks (shet marks) *n*
Those funny looking lines that show up on your nails if you polish them after 8 pm.

Shopping (shop•peng) *n*
A duty to be performed to ensure a viable
and stable economic condition in the
global marketplace i.e., "Honey, I'm
going out to strengthen the economy."

Shower (shou•er) *n*
1) An area of the bathroom usually bordered by a horizontal bar designed to support a shower curtain and drying nylons, or
2) A gathering of women that includes gifts and silly party games.

Sidewalk Grate (sid•wok grat) *n*
A high heel catcher.

Significant Other
(sig•nif•i•kant uth•er) *n*
A husband, fiancé, live-in boyfriend, or
someone you've actually introduced to
your parents.

Single (sing•gl) *adj*
What your boyfriend of one year better
not refer to himself as.

Soap Opera (sop op•ra) *n*
A daytime television show you become
emotionally involved with to help you
appreciate the fact that you don't have the
same problems to become emotionally
involved with in the first place.

Some Assembly Required
(komp•li•ka•ted) *adj*
Means you need a master's degree in
engineering to it put together.

Space (spas) *n*
When used with "I need my," code words
for "I've met someone else."

Stress (stres) *n*

Mr. Webster says "physical, mental or emotional strain." Mrs. Webster agrees, especially when the phone rings, the baby cries, the television blares and the doorbell rings all at the same time — usually five minutes after she was supposed to leave for work.

Stretch Marks (linz) *n*
Badges of honor.

Stud (stud) *n*
Something to help you hang pictures.

Sweatsuit (swet•soot) *n*
All-purpose clothing for weekends.

Mrs. Webster's Dictionary

Taxing (taks•eng) *adj*
Mr. Webster says "Burdensome,
wearing." Mrs. Webster says "See IRS."

Teddy Bear (ted•ee baer) *n*
A companion who gives you a hug whenever you want, never snores, doesn't bother you when you're talking on the phone and doesn't eat the last chocolate chip cookie.

Thanksgiving (thangks•giv•eng) *n*
A holiday where you have to choose
between dinner at his parents, dinner at
your parents, or the compromise of
eating two full turkey dinners.

Thermostat (thur•ma•stat) *n*
The mechanism that controls the
temperature in the house; a bone of
contention similar to the remote control.

Mrs. Webster's Dictionary

Three (thre) *n*
When he's watching TV, the minimum number of times you have to call his name before he realizes you are talking to him.

Toilet Seat (toi•lit seet) *n*
What Mr. Webster never remembers to
put down.

Twenty-nine (twen•tee nin) *n*
The "phantom year" when no one
believes that is really your age.

Valentine's Day (val•en•tinez dae) *n*
A day when you have dreams of a
candlelight dinner, diamonds and
romance, but consider yourself lucky to
get a card.

Waterproof Mascara (mas•kar•a) *n*
Comes off if you cry, shower, or swim,
but not if you try to remove it.

Wedding (wed•eng) *n*
A one hour ceremony which requires
18 months of preparation and the
participants are too nervous to
remember afterwards.

Weight Lifting (wate lif•ting) *n*
What every women does when she carries
her baby, purse and two bags of groceries.

Work (werk) *n*
The hum-drum stuff that interrupts coffee breaks, lunches, shopping and personal phone calls.

Working Women (wer•king wim•en) *n*
All of us. See "Redundant."

Yippee (yip•pee) *interj*
What a woman thinks when a man says
he'll call — then does.

Zillion (zil•ycn) n
The number of times you ask someone to take out the trash, then end up doing it yourself anyway.

OTHER TITLES BY GREAT QUOTATIONS PUBLISHING COMPANY

199 Useful Things to Do With A Politician
201 Best Things Ever Said
A Lifetime of Love
A Light Heart Lives Long
A Teacher Is Better Than Two Books
As A Cat Thinketh
Cheatnotes On Life
Chicken Soup
Dear Mr. President
Father Knows Best
Food For Thought
Golden Years, Golden Words
Happiness Walks On Busy Feet
Heal The World
Hooked on Golf
Hollywords

In Celebration of Women
Life's Simple Pleasures
For Mother - A Bouquet of Sentiment
Motivation Magic
Mrs. Webster's Dictionary
I'm Not Over The Hill ...
Reflections
Romantic Rendezvous
Sports Page
So Many Ways To Say Thank You
The ABC's of Parenting
The Best Of Friends
The Birthday Astrologer
The Little Book of Spiritual Wisdom
Things You'll Learn, If You Live Long Enough

GREAT QUOTATIONS PUBLISHING CO.

1967 Quincy Court
Glendale Heights, IL 60139-2045
Phone (708) 582-2800
FAX (708) 582-2813